J

 **ISLINGTON**

South Library
115-117 Essex Road
London N1 2SL
Tel: 020 7527 7860

Library & Cultural Services

This item should be returned on or before the last date stamped below.
Users who do not return items promptly may be liable to overdue charges.
When renewing items please quote the number on your membership card.

01/09

2 4 SEP 2009

16 FEB 2009

-7 NOV 2009   1 5 DEC 2012

13 MAR 2009   2 8 DEC 2012

30 JAN 2010

-1 SEP 2011   -5 DEC 2011   08 APR 2013

27 MAR 2012

-1 SEP 2011   0 1 MAY 2012

1 0 SEP 2012

Lib.1

The life cycle of an Apple

Ruth Thomson

WAYLAND

First published in 2008 by Wayland,
a division of Hachette Children's Books

Copyright © Wayland 2008

Wayland
338 Euston Road
London NW1 3BH

Wayland Australia
Level 17/207 Kent Street
Sydney, NSW 2000

Editor: Clare Lewis
Designer: Simon Morse
Consultant: Michael Scott OBE, B.Sc

Photographs: 8 Mark Boulton Photography/Alamy; Cover
(br), 20 Elizabeth Czitronyi/Alamy; Cover (main)
Phil Degginger/Alamy; Cover (tr), 9, 10, 23 (tl) Holt Studios
International Ltd/Nigel Cattin/Alamy; 14 isifa Image
Service s.r.o./Alamy; 3, 4, 5, 6, 7, 11, 12, 13, 15,
16, 17, 18, 19, 21, 22 naturepl.com

British Library Cataloguing in Publication Data
Thomson, Ruth
    The life cycle of an apple. - (Learning about
life cycles)
    1. Apples - Life cycles - Juvenile literature
    I. Title
    583.7'3
ISBN-13: 978-0-7502-5596-7

Printed and bound in China

Wayland is a division of Hachette Children's
Books, an Hachette Livre UK company
www.hachettelivre.co.uk

Contents

Apples grow here

Apples grow on apple trees. Sometimes you can see apple trees in gardens. Farmers plant trees in rows in grassy fields. These are called orchards.

What is an apple?

Apples are a delicious **fruit**. They can be red, green, brown or yellow. They can taste crisp, soft, sweet, tangy, juicy or dry.

Apples have a thin skin
and a fleshy inside.
The **core** in the centre
has dark **seeds** called pips.

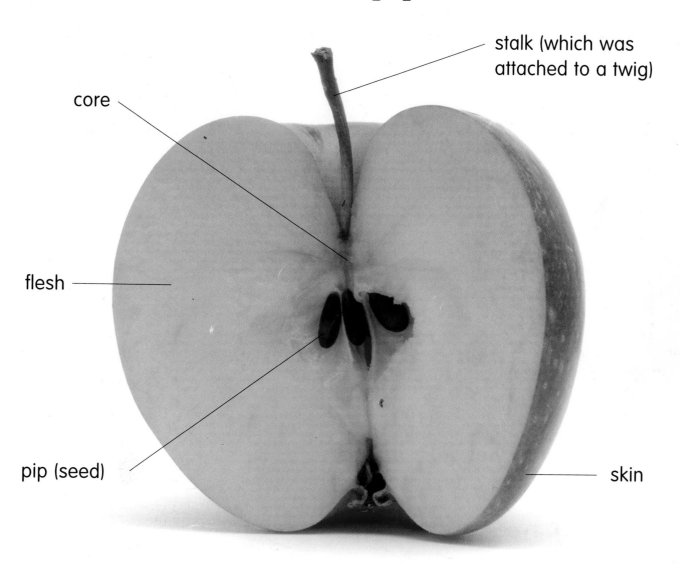

stalk (which was
attached to a twig)

core

flesh

pip (seed)

skin

7

Apple trees

Apple farmers look after their trees to make sure they get lots of healthy **fruit**.

In winter, they cut back some of the branches. This helps the tree to grow well. It also helps light to reach the leaves and fruit.

Buds

In spring, new flowers and leaves appear. At first they are tightly closed. They are called **buds**. The leaf buds open first.

May

On the end of each leafy
twig are pink flower buds.
When the tree is covered
with leaves, these buds
open into flowers
called blossom.

Flowers

The blossom has white and pink petals and a sweet smell. It also has a sweet liquid called **nectar** and a yellow powder called **pollen**.

petal

pollen

The scent of the blossom
attracts bees to the flowers.
They come to feed on
the sweet nectar.

Pollination

Pollen sticks to the bee
when it feeds on **nectar**.

July

When the bee flies to another flower, pollen from the first flower rubs off on to the next one. This is called pollination.

Apples

When a flower is pollinated, **seeds** grow inside it. The flower is no longer needed, so its petals drop off.

A tiny apple starts swelling around the seeds. It grows bigger and bigger all summer.

August

Ripe and ready

By autumn, the apples are sweeter and more colourful. They are **ripe** and ready to eat.

September

The apple tree is ready for picking. Sometimes, branches are so heavy with apples, they bend right down to the ground.

Autumn and winter

In autumn, as the days get shorter and colder, the leaves change colour. Soon, they fall off the tree.

November

The tree rests with its branches
bare, all winter long. New **buds**
appear on every twig.

May

Spring

In spring, the weather warms up again. Leaves and then blossom appear. By summer, new apples will start growing.

Apple life cycle

Buds
In spring, **buds** swell and leaves appear.

Flowers
When the tree is covered with leaves, blossom appears.

Fruit
Apples are **ripe** and ready for picking.

Seeds
Seeds grow in pollinated flowers. Tiny apples start growing.

Glossary

bud part of a tree from which leaves or flowers develop

core centre part of an apple

fruit part of a flowering plant that holds its seeds

nectar sweet liquid inside many flowers that attracts insects

pollen grains of powder in flowers needed to make new seeds

ripe when the apple is sweet and ready to eat

seed part of a plant that grows into a new plant

Index